Carine MacKenzie

Illustrated by F

CW01401359

So, What is the Gospel?

The Gospel is Good News.

It is the message sent by God to all people in the world – that means you too. The Bible is God's special message to us. God wants to tell us about himself, and how we should please him. He did this by giving us a book. Many different people were told by God what to write, but God is the author.

The Bible is true. It
is called the truth
of God.

God had no beginning and will have no end.

He is eternal. That is difficult to understand because we understand things as they exist in time and space. The first words of the Bible are: 'In the beginning God made the heavens and the earth.'

He made every part of the world and everything in it by the word of his power.

God spoke and it was done.
What a marvellous powerful God!

God made the first man, Adam, and Eve, his wife.

They lived happily in the Garden of Eden, but soon sin entered their lives. Satan, the evil one, in the form of a serpent tempted Eve to take some fruit that God had told them not to eat. Adam joined her in that disobedience.

Adam and Eve became sinners and were no longer perfectly happy. They were punished and put out of the beautiful garden. Life became difficult. Pain and sorrow became part of their life.

Every person born since then has the same problem – sin which brings sadness and difficulty and deserves God's punishment.

God provided an answer to this problem of sin.

Because God loved the world he had made so much, he promised to send a Saviour for his people.

Throughout the Old Testament, the first thirty-nine books of the Bible, God mentions the one who would come to save his people from their sins.

Advance information was given – he would be born in Bethlehem, his mother would be a virgin, he would belong to the tribe of Judah, the family of David. All the people of Israel who had read God's Word were waiting for the coming Saviour.

Then the promises came true. Jesus was born in Bethlehem to Mary who was a virgin. Bethlehem was the city of David.

Angels from heaven announced the birth of Jesus to some shepherds. The shepherds found the baby wrapped up, lying in a manger. They fell down and worshipped him.

This little baby was the promised Saviour.

God told Joseph, Mary's husband, to call the baby, Jesus, which means 'Saviour', for he shall save his people from their sins.

Jesus is God, the Son.

He came to this world as a human being. He lived
a perfect life. He did not sin, he taught the people
wisely. He healed sick people and showed great
kindness to many poor people. He always did what
pleased God, the Father. His life was not one of ease
and wealth. Some wicked men plotted to kill him.
They made wicked plans. Jesus was arrested and
sentenced to death. But God's plans are better and
higher than any other plans.

Jesus was taken to Calvary outside the city of Jerusalem. There, his hands and feet were nailed to a cross. He hung on the cross until he died. His death was painful and shameful, but he took it willingly.

Jesus' death was part of God the Father's plan to save his people from their sins.

Jesus took the punishment for sin, not his own sin for he did not have any, but for the sin of his people. His people are those who trust in him, those whom God has chosen to be his own.

God so loved the world that he sent his Son to die on the cross so that those who believe on him, and trust him, would not have to suffer eternal punishment in hell for their sin. Instead they would have everlasting life in heaven.

Jesus' body was buried in a tomb. A big stone covered the entrance. On the third day, after his death, some friends went to visit the tomb. They found the stone rolled away.

The tomb was empty. An angel spoke to them. 'You are looking for Jesus. He is risen from the dead.'

Many people met the risen Lord Jesus in the following days. His special friends met him on several occasions, and up to 500 people saw him at one time. Jesus ascended up into heaven while his friends were watching. His body was lifted up through the clouds.

Jesus will return again to judge the world, we are told. No one knows when that will be.

God asks us to repent. That means we are to be sorry for our sin and to turn away from it to God. Those who trust in the Lord Jesus have their sins forgiven because of his death on the cross. They have the peace of God in their hearts. They have real lasting joy in their lives.

Life is different for those who trust in Jesus because he makes the difference.

God speaks to us in the Bible.

He wants us to speak to him. We do this by praying to him. If we love Jesus, praying is like speaking to a best friend. We can tell him how much we love him. We can say sorry for the wrong things we have thought, or said or done. We can thank God for all the good things he has given us and done for us. We can ask him to help us with any problem or situation.

After Jesus returned to heaven, his followers with the special help of God the Holy Spirit, started to preach the Good News wherever they could. 'Jesus Christ died for the ungodly.'

'Jesus died to save his people from their sin.'

'The Wages of sin is death, but the gift of God is eternal life through Jesus Christ.'

What good news!

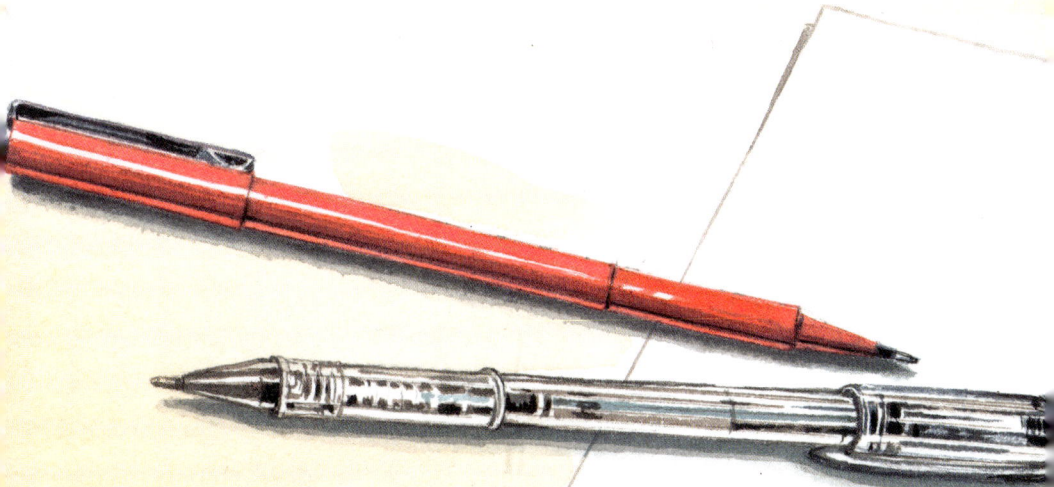

Sin deserves the wrath of God in hell; but God gave the gift of life for ever in heaven with Jesus, to those who trust in him.

Jesus has done it all. We have nothing to do to earn this wonderful gift of salvation.

If we love God, we will want to live in a way that is pleasing to him. However, many times we will fail. We should read God's Word every day. We should pray to him often We should worship God in his house, the church, with other people who love him too.

We should try to tell others the Good News of Salvation through Jesus Christ.

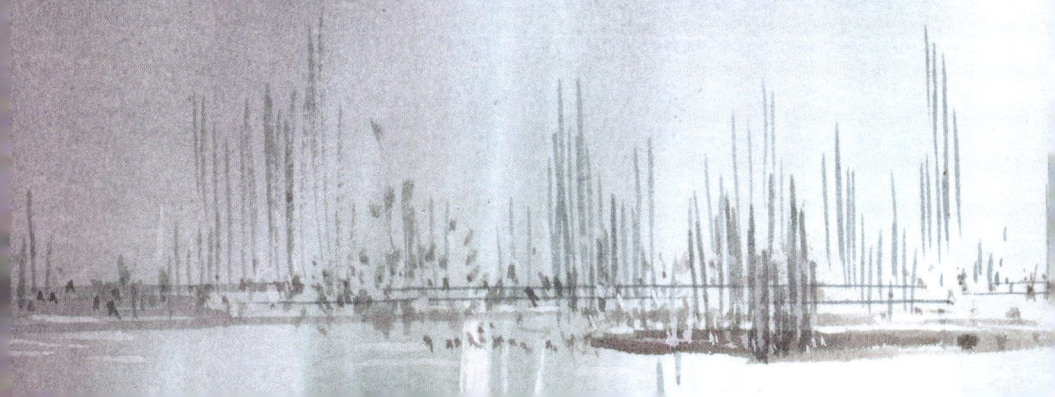

CHRISTIAN FOCUS PUBLICATIONS

Christian Focus Publications publishes books for adults and children under its four main imprints: Christian Focus, CF4K, Mentor and Christian Heritage. Our books reflect our conviction that God's Word is reliable and Jesus is the way to know him, and live for ever with him. Our children's list includes a Sunday School curriculum that covers pre-school to early teens, and puzzle and activity books. We also publish personal and family devotional titles, biographies and inspirational stories that children will love. If you are looking for quality Bible teaching for children, then we have an excellent range of Bible stories and age-specific theological books. From pre-school board books to teenage apologetics, we have it covered!

10 9 8 7 6 5 4 3 2 1
Copyright © 2019 Carine Mackenzie
ISBN:978-1-5271-0307-8
Published by Christian Focus Publications, Geanies House, Fearn, Tain, Ross-shire, IV20 1TW, U.K.
Illustrations by Fred Apps; Cover design by Daniel van Straaten
Printed in Malta

Scripture quotations are the authors own paraphrase.

All rights reserved. No part of this publication may be reproduced, stored in a retrieval system, or transmitted, in any form, by any means, electronic, mechanical, photocopying, recording or otherwise without the prior permission of the publisher or a licence permitting restricted copying. In the U.K. such licences are issued by the Copyright Licensing Agency, Saffron House, 6-10 Kirby Street, London, EC1 8TS. www.cla.co.uk